GW00776055

25 VIEWS OF DUBLIN
JAMES HORAN

Commentary Benedict Kiely

Essay Peter Somerville-Large

Town House, Dublin
in association with
The Office of Public Works

 OPW

Published in 1994 by
Town House and Country House
Trinity House
Charleston Road
Ranelagh, Dublin 6
Ireland

in association with
The Office of Public Works

A CIP catalogue record for this book is
available from the British Library

ISBN: 0-948524-16-2

Front cover: *College Green* by
James Horan
Back cover: *Casino at Marino* by
James Horan

Design: Bill Murphy
Origination: The Kulor Centre, Dublin
Printed in Ireland by ßetaprint

Author's acknowledgements
The Horan prints would not have been possible without the assistance and
support of many individuals. I would like to thank successive Ministers of
State with responsibility for the Office of Public Works who commissioned
and showed a continuous interest in this project. In particular I would like
to thank the present Minister of State Noel Dempsey TD, Government
Chief Whip, who launched the complete series in the Taylor Galleries in
June 1994. Special thanks is due to the Commissioners of Public Works
under their chairman John Mahony, and the Art Management Committee,
chaired by Commissioner Brian Murphy, and its members, Michael
O'Doherty, director of architectural services, Noel de Chenu, art adviser,
Angela Rolfe, architect, William Gallagher, former curator of the Glebe
Gallery, Christine Sisk and Mary Heffernan. The advice of the Arts Council
is also acknowledged.

Copyright acknowledgements
The publishers would like to thank the following for permission to
reproduce copyright material: The Trustees of the Estate of Patrick
Kavanagh, C/o Peter Fallon, Literary Agent, Loughcrew, Oldcastle,
Co Meath, Ireland, for excerpts from Patrick Kavanagh's poems, and Faber
and Faber Ltd for excerpt from 'Dublin' by Louis MacNeice from *Collected
Poems by Louis MacNeice*, edited by E R Dobbs.

CONTENTS

PREFACE   *6*

PAINTING DUBLIN   *7*

LOCATION MAPS   *11*

1. GRAFTON STREET   *14*

2. CUSTOM HOUSE   *16*

3. TRINITY COLLEGE   *18*

4. PORTOBELLO   *20*

5. CHRISTCHURCH CATHEDRAL   *22*

6. HEUSTON STATION   *24*

7. NATIONAL CONCERT HALL   *26*

8. FRUIT AND VEGETABLE MARKET   *28*

9. GOVERNMENT BUILDINGS   *30*

10. ST PATRICK'S CATHEDRAL   *32*

11. DAME STREET   *34*

12. BUSARAS   *36*

13. DUBLIN CASTLE   *38*

14. THE FOUR COURTS   *40*

15. GRAND CANAL PLACE   *42*

16. GRAND CANAL DOCK   *44*

17. COLLEGE GREEN   *46*

18. WESTLAND ROW   *48*

19. O'CONNELL STREET   *50*

20. ROTUNDA, PARNELL STREET   *52*

21. ST GEORGE'S CHURCH   *54*

22. CIVIC OFFICES, WOOD QUAY   *56*

23. CASINO AT MARINO   *58*

24. DÚN LAOGHAIRE HARBOUR   *60*

25. DUBLIN AIRPORT   *62*

P R E F A C E

In 1991, as part of the celebration of Dublin's role as the European City of Culture, the Office of Public Works commissioned a set of twenty-five drawings that would depict the city as it appears at the end of the twentieth century. I was honoured to be invited to execute this commission.

My first and possibly most difficult task was to adopt an attitude to the project, both in the selection of the twenty-five views and in determining to what extent the drawings should include some of the more unsightly elements of a modern urban environment — elements ranging from the road markings and street signs to areas of dereliction and buildings of unsympathetic architectural character.

Two hundred years previously, James Malton produced the first of his twenty-five drawings of Dublin, giving an architect's and artist's view of the city at the end of the eighteenth century. Though many of Malton's buildings still remain, the city of Dublin today is a very different place from what it was in 1790. It has expanded far beyond its Georgian boundaries and the lifestyle and activities of its inhabitants have undergone considerable change.

Bearing in mind these variables, it was decided that the contemporary views of the city should be just that — showing the city as it is now. Nevertheless, the remaining buildings from Malton's collection would appear where possible, even in the role of 'supporting actors' to the layers of architectural history that make up Dublin today.

There followed a three-year period of walking the city, sketching and photographing and gradually assembling the material that would form the basis of the final set of drawings. The work was carried out at all hours of day and night and the city was observed and recorded through its changing seasons.

Even as the drawings were being completed, changes were taking place within the city. The gasometer, seen in the drawing of the Custom House (No 2), disappeared, and the new Civic Offices were constructed between the period of drawing the Four Courts (No 14) and Woodquay and Christchurch (No 22). This particular drawing has an interesting parallel with Malton's work. He portrayed the Four Courts before the building was completed and his drawing suggests significant conjecture. Normally an artist portraying unfinished buildings would have obtained assistance from the architect, but due to bad feeling between Malton and Gandon, this assistance may not have been forthcoming and, consequently, major discrepancies exist between Malton's drawing and the finished building. In contrast, Scott Tallon Walker, architects for the Civic Offices, provided all the necessary information to allow me to complete the drawing some nine months before the building itself was completed.

Another interesting relationship exists between the drawing of the Casino at Marino and Malton's drawing of College Green. His drawing includes a man in a green jacket and yellow breeches crossing the road carrying a stick. Apparently, in the original the man was conducting a pig across the road. The City Fathers of the time considered it inappropriate to have a pig appear in front of the Houses of Parliament — now the Bank of Ireland — and so the pig was duly erased. In the drawing of the Casino at Marino, the man with the green jacket and yellow breeches returns complete with pig, making a small reference to Malton's original intention.

The drawings contain many other references to contemporary people and events, which are not identified but are there for the keen observer to find.

On average, each drawing took almost sixty hours to complete, excluding the time spent sketching and the research work on the street. This represents a total average time of two hours every day for three years. It has been a particular pleasure and privilege to have carried out this commission, apart from the fact that it has extended my knowledge and understanding of my adopted city.

J F H

PAINTING DUBLIN

When James Malton produced his *Picturesque and Descriptive View of the City of Dublin*, he was recording a sophisticated Georgian city at its apotheosis. His twenty-five views have given succeeding generations compelling and evocative glimpses of a wonderful Georgian metropolis. They form a record of what Jonah Barrington, writing nostalgically several decades later, considered the 'Golden Age' of Dublin.

Two centuries later, James Horan has made a contemporary record of the city that Malton observed so painstakingly. Over three years Horan has painted a new set of 'descriptive' cityscapes using similar skills — a blend of architectural and social observation that complements the famous views of his namesake. He has not been afraid to depict similar scenes to those painted by Malton, such as the Custom House, the Rotunda and Trinity College. Dublin Castle is shown with its new twentieth-century embellishments. Among the views he has chosen to retain is Lord Charlemont's exquisite Casino at Clontarf, a pure classical pleasure to any student of architecture. In addition, he includes a series of paintings which indicate changes that have taken place over two hundred years. The post-Malton buildings include Victorian landmarks and major works of contemporary architects. In the 1990s, James Horan, like James Malton before him,

presents us with a celebration of Dublin.

The works of both artists demonstrate the architectural training essential for successful topographical drawing. When Malton depicted the Custom House, James Gandon's great public building erected on swamp land, he showed it in all its elegance sloping down the Liffey, with every detail of its façade carefully recorded. In front, the viewer can examine the bustle of Liffey commerce — lighters, row boats, ships anchored on what appears to be a sunny day, bystanders, merchants, and a number of barrels, perhaps of porter.

It seems appropriate that this print is one of the most familiar of Malton's views. An Englishman, born in 1760, Malton came to Ireland as a young draughtsman and worked for Gandon during the long troubled building of the Custom House, which lasted over a decade. After that he began to record the most prominent buildings in Dublin. His views were drawn in 1790 and 1791 and published in parts during the following eight years. They were completed and had already become popular before his tragic death by suicide in 1803. By then he had departed for London and the post-Union gloom was upon the city he had depicted at its most glorious.

The slow process of etching, aquatint and engraving began with his watercolour drawings, which were printed in sepia and black. The prints were then hand-coloured

by colourists following his instructions. He also did a number of watercolour copies. The views continued to be published up until 1820, by which date the plates had become very worn. There was a time when nearly every doctor and dentist in Dublin had a few Maltons displayed in the waiting-room. From many a dentist's chair the patient could look out to a skyline of dusty Georgian brick similar to Malton's outlines. Their popularity has continued.

Malton wrote: 'Dublin is the second city in his Britannic Majesty's dominions and may rank with the very finest cities of Europe for extent, magnificence and commerce.' Outside London, Dublin was a centre for theatre, music and publishing. Many Englishmen seeking opportunities emigrated there. Irish aristocracy was at its peak in the years leading up to the 1798 rebellion. The great buildings exemplify classical architecture at its grandest. The façade of Trinity College, its library, the domed barrel of the Four Courts, the Rotunda, the Parliament buildings — all are depicted with elegance and truth.

Malton's views are not only valuable as an architectural record. Following the convention of the times, Malton showed glimpses of everyday life, not just society's ladies and fops, but also the poor and needy. The elegance was accompanied by a darker side of life.

Outside Parliament House stands a red-coated soldier with crossed bandoliers and high bonnet, as fashionable ladies casting long shadows walk past. Once there were two pigs loitering by the steps. Most people know how Malton painted them out and changed them into a solitary dog. The story that the House of Commons, mindful of its dignity, insisted on the change, may, however, be apocryphal. But those pigs hint at an earthy, ramshackle, poverty-stricken life that seethed beside the engaged columns and Corinthian façades of the noble newly constructed public buildings. The French traveller de Latocnaye, who came to Dublin about this time, found 'a very gloomy and dirty city' and added that 'you are every moment stopped by funerals, droves of cattle, or beggars, who go through the streets by dozens, and yet this city is one of the richest and most commercial in Europe'.

Malton did not let poverty spoil his prints, but continually hinted at it. Outside St Catherine's Church a notice indicates the consolation of the poor: 'Rum, Brandy, Mead, Whiskey, Arrack Wholesale and Retail. Publican Dennis Plunket.' According to a survey there were two thousand ale-houses, three hundred taverns and twelve hundred brandy shops in Dublin in the 1790s. Opposite the Rotunda a beggar holds out his cap, while another is stationed near the Tholsel. Both a blind man and a beggar haunt Capel Street outside two of the city's numerous lottery offices. In his *Letters to the Irish Nation* George Cooper described how they 'are generally papered with green and gold and lighted up with a profusion of most expensive cut glass chandeliers . . . . In these shops are crowds of the most miserable ragged objects . . . staking their daily bread on the chance of gain'. Tickets for the draw

were selected from drums by two boys from the Blue Coat School, the subject of another of the views. Perhaps those who run the modern lottery can get a few ideas from the eighteenth-century model.

When Malton drew Capel Street, Essex Bridge was still the centre of the city. Soon the axis wound eastward to Carlisle Bridge which was completed in 1798; the scaffolding that covered it was used as an impromptu gallows during the rebellion. Previously ships sailed up to Essex Bridge, and one is seen leaning in the Liffey mud. The old Custom House, visible on the far bank, was already out of use, as Gandon's brand new version had been completed after many turbulent years.

Beyond the Palladian west front of Trinity College can be glimpsed the Provost's house. In front walks a lady and her two children, a poor woman and her toddler and a groom leading his horse. Other strollers pass by the railings, while at the north end a woman has set up a fruit stall, not unlike the women of Moore Street today. Glimpses of hucksters in other Malton prints include a tallow chandler's shop in Thomas Street, beside the Tholsel, and the ramshackle butcher's stalls at the west door of St Patrick's Cathedral.

Another representation of St Patrick's, which contains much melancholy contemplation of tombstones, is particularly valuable as an historical document since the cathedral's mouldering early Gothic would be transformed almost beyond recognition by Sir Thomas Drew, who, subsidised by Sir Benjamin Lee Guinness, rebuilt most of it.

Every print has social and topographical detail which enables Malton's work to remain a record, sanitised to some extent, of life in the eighteenth-century city. We can examine merchants on horseback, soldiers,

gossiping countrymen, women at open windows, and a couple of chairmen at the specially built sedan stop outside Lord Charlemont's house. Scholars in Trinity library stand below rows of leather-bound books. The inevitable beggars were a Dublin phenomenon that revolted travellers. The Frenchman, de Latocnaye, observed that 'The splendid carriages and the apparent wealth of the principal houses render the more displeasing the sight of the beggars . . . they may be seen hanging on for hours to the railings of basements, forcing charity by depriving those who live in these places of light and air'. Placing a beggar in a formal Dublin scene was nothing new. Francis Wheatley sketched a beggar under the portico of the House of Commons in 1782. An early eighteenth-century print of Dublin Bay shows a group of beggars at Beggar's Bush, where country vagrants traditionally assembled before making their descent on the city.

Many of the buildings Malton drew have survived, although there have been inevitable changes. Like St Patrick's, the Custom House and the Four Courts, battered during the Civil War, have been largely rebuilt. Others have changed identity. Thomas Ivory's King's Hospital in Blackhall Place, alias the Blue Coat School, is now the headquarters of the Incorporated Law Society, the governing body of the solicitors' profession. Lord Charlemont's magnificent town house has become the Municipal Gallery.

A few city landmarks have disappeared altogether. The arcaded Tholsel, or town hall, already ruinous when Malton drew it, was demolished in 1806. (It bore some resemblance to the Tholsel that survives in Kilkenny High Street.) Thomas Cooley's Hibernian Marine School, wrongly attributed by Malton to Thomas Ivory, housed 180 boys aged between nine and fourteen who received an education that qualified them for the British Navy or Mercantile Marine. This was pulled down as recently as 1979.

I am old enough to remember being taken around St Stephen's Green by my nanny at a time when John van Nost's fine equestrian statue of King George II stood in what is now a plain flowerbed. Soon after, King George was a victim of statue-politics; but in those days he looked through the encircling trees towards the warm tinted glow of the surrounding Georgian houses. Malton drew him surrounded by ladies and gentlemen of fashion strolling on the gravel paths; over the centuries Stephen's Green has remained a fashionable focal point.

In the 1930s there were still social links back to Malton's Dublin. I lived in a graceful house near Fitzwilliam Square, which like others in that Georgian part of Dublin was still privately owned. From my nursery window on the top floor I could see the barrel organman on his regular visits, and once a man leading a shuffling bear on a chain. At the back of the house, barges were being pulled by horses along the canal; most deliveries were by horse-drawn vans. In the kitchen, tucked away in the basement, reached by a cold flight of stairs, the cook attended a great cast iron stove fed by coals which came down from overhead shutes in the street outside.

I grew up in a Dublin where the genteel and rarified atmosphere of the squares and the smart suburbs went side by side with the slums and tenements described by O'Casey. The changes that have taken place since then are greater than those that occurred between the Act of Union and the post-Treaty period.

But change was inevitable from the moment Malton put down his pen. Little more than thirty years after his death, the post-Union city had become part of the bustling Victorian world. There were new buildings, many still classical like the pro-Cathedral and the General Post Office. New bridges were built across the Liffey. The Grand Canal running through Ringsend and Portobello on the south side and the Royal Canal making for Dublin Bay and Mountjoy Square on the north side provided a service that had reached its twilight years. Soon the canals would be extinguished by the railways, James Horan's quiet perspective of the Grand Canal with its Guinness barge seldom viewed by Dubliner or visitor, contrasting with the commercial bustle of Malton's Custom House. The nerve centre of commerce and transport has long moved away from water.

Horan's paintings include some of the most imposing nineteenth-century buildings. The classical façade of Francis Johnston's General Post Office is attended by Oisín Kelly's vivid bronze of the Labour leader Jim Larkin. Among his views of Victorian buildings is a meticulous record of Sancton Wood's Kingsbridge Station, now renamed Heuston Station, which Maurice Craig considered 'delightful, a renaissance *palazzo*, gay and full-blooded'. The railway reappears in the view of Westland Row. Another familiar *palazzo*, which Horan has drawn with a couple of substantial yachts anchored in front, is the Royal Irish Yacht Club at Dún Laoghaire.

Dublin was always under threat of change and decay. James Joyce failed to see it through Malton's rose-coloured spectacles. (Malton would scarcely have approved of Joyce's description of Trinity as 'a dull stone set in the city's ring'.) The young journalist V S Pritchett wrote at the time of the Civil War: 'Dublin is being pulled down or is falling down . . . in street after street the wreckers are pulling [it] down.' 'You've come just in time', people told him, 'in a few year's time there will be little of eighteenth- and nineteenth-century Dublin left.'

Like the statues, the old Georgian buildings came to represent a society and class that had little to do with Ireland. Republican triumphalism despised the glories of Malton's Dublin. Many people can remember the plight of the Tailor's Hall and other famous buildings that were allowed to deteriorate. Others were victims of neglect, prejudice and commercial greed. As late as the 1960s it seemed that the heart of the Georgian city would be erased.

The miracle is that so much has been saved. This has been a result of a combination of economic improvement and changing attitudes. Today it would be unlikely that a whole eighteenth-century street would be pulled down to make way for offices. A government minister would hesitate before condemning Georgian buildings for being associated with belted earls. They are no longer seen as evidence of Saxon conquest, but as an achievement in which all Irish people can take pride. Irish Georgian buildings are different from those elsewhere. Irish craftsmen, stuccadores and carpenters, many trained in the old Hibernian school, brought an invigorating panache to contemporary style.

In recent years the Royal Hospital has been magnificently restored. The classical front of the Bank of Ireland, the Parliament Building of Malton's day, has been stripped of the grime of centuries, and Trinity College is also being cleaned. On the north

9

side of the city, many of the houses in North Great George's Street and Henrietta Street which were derelict a few years ago are now being lovingly restored. Lord Charlemont's Casino shines out like a beacon among the suburbs of Clontarf. Buck Whaley's house, now part of the National University, has been brought back to life. Today one can walk through avenues of red-brick Georgian terraces, newly cleaned and restored, and feel at home with James Malton's Dublin.

James Horan's Dublin is equally vibrant. He refuses to be confined to important buildings of one particular era so that the mix presented in his twenty-five post-Malton views correctly reflects recent architectural achievement. Horan's technique echoes Malton's without imitating it. Malton's interior of the Trinity College library is neatly contrasted by Horan's National Concert Hall, where orchestra and audience are assembled with mathematical precision beneath generously columnated spaces of the transformed University College Examination Hall.

Horan's contemporary social detail includes the bustle of the city's fruit and vegetable markets, office workers, shoppers and strollers and the movement on the tarmac outside the airport building on a rainy day. The aeroplane standing on wet tarmac complements the tenders and sailing ships outside Malton's Custom House. Nor is he afraid of the car. So much modern topographical work gives the impression of being drawn at five o'clock on a summer's morning when every vehicle is in its garage. His view of Dame Street includes a fine Dublin traffic jam not far from where Malton's pigs sauntered. By contrast, the view of Grafton Street from the south end emphasises the changes since the old traffic-

torn days before the pedestrian precinct provided an area of leisure and recreation.

In the foreground of Dame Street is the portico of the Bank of Ireland. In the background, Horan uses the blend of old and new that he loves by showing Sam Stephenson's truncated Central Bank. This tower, which has incurred the dislike of many Dubliners, manages to loom over the cityscape. Stephenson appears in another view where his Civic Offices stand beside Christchurch Cathedral. Today the cathedral would be almost unrecognisable to Malton in view of its comprehensive rebuilding in the 1870s by the Gothic Revival architect George Edmund Street.

Another twentieth-century building chosen by Horan is Michael Scott's innovative Bus Station, completed in 1953, the first essay in modern architecture that has left its stamp on the city. He paints the Rotunda attended by Augustus St Gaudens' moving monument to Charles Stewart Parnell which stands at the north end of O'Connell Street, offering a little recompense for the vanished Nelson's Pillar that made O'Connell Street one of the most imposing thoroughfares on these islands.

His Custom House is shown from a similar prospect to Malton's, only more sharply angled. (The nineteenth-century Loop Line Bridge impedes any view of Gandon's masterpiece from the west.) A rowing eight moves down the Liffey. In the distance is the gasometer, which used to be visible over much of Dublin, including Merrion Square, and was as familiar as Nelson's Pillar used to be forty years ago. Here is an example of the ever-changing city, a record of the past; since Horan made his painting the gasometer has been pulled down.

Another fragile landmark whose future remains in doubt is Francis Johnston's fine St George's Church, which like many redundant Protestant churches has not found another role. Recently its eighteenth-century pews were sold off. The Government Offices in Merrion Street have had better fortune. The external facelift alone has changed a group of dour and shabby buildings into a gleaming nerve centre of government.

Dublin is not only blessed by the architecture depicted by Malton and Horan. There can be few capital cities where the natural attractions of sea and land combine to give such dominance. From Howth Head to Bray around the wide curve of Dublin Bay the city is dominated by its undulating mountains. As Pritchett wrote: 'Dublin captivates by the purity and languor of its air and the beauty of its situation.' From Killiney the young Bernard Shaw watched the changing formation of clouds which all his life he considered unequalled in beauty to those elsewhere.

How long does it take to walk through the heart of Dublin? A matter of minutes or a couple of centuries?

Peter Somerville-Large

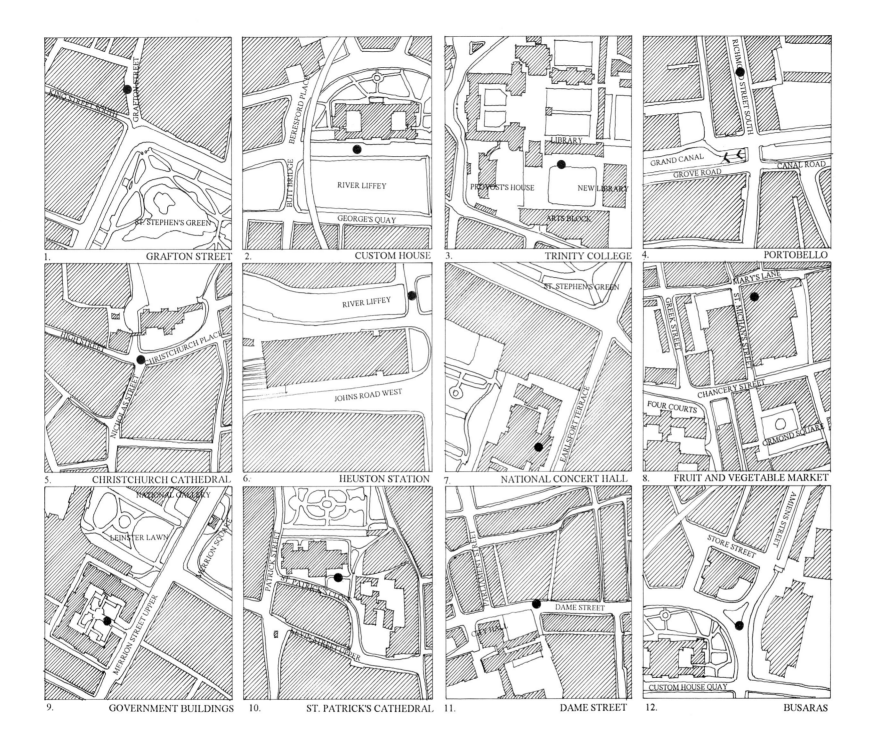

1.   GRAFTON STREET   2.   CUSTOM HOUSE   3.   TRINITY COLLEGE   4.   PORTOBELLO

5.   CHRISTCHURCH CATHEDRAL   6.   HEUSTON STATION   7.   NATIONAL CONCERT HALL   8.   FRUIT AND VEGETABLE MARKET

9.   GOVERNMENT BUILDINGS   10.   ST. PATRICK'S CATHEDRAL   11.   DAME STREET   12.   BUSARAS

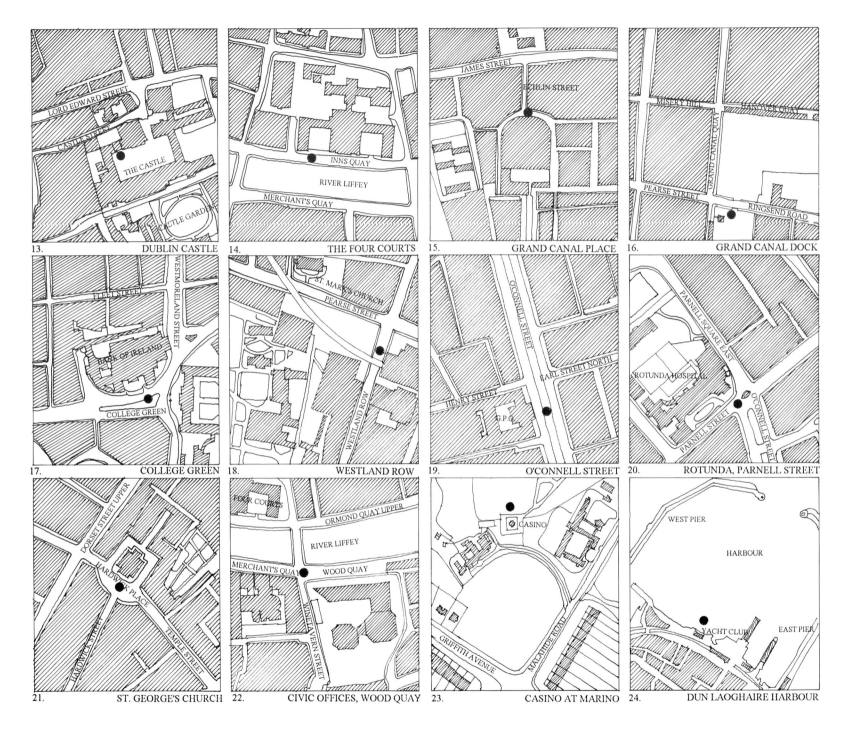

13.   DUBLIN CASTLE   14.   THE FOUR COURTS   15.   GRAND CANAL PLACE   16.   GRAND CANAL DOCK

17.   COLLEGE GREEN   18.   WESTLAND ROW   19.   O'CONNELL STREET   20.   ROTUNDA, PARNELL STREET

21.   ST. GEORGE'S CHURCH   22.   CIVIC OFFICES, WOOD QUAY   23.   CASINO AT MARINO   24.   DUN LAOGHAIRE HARBOUR

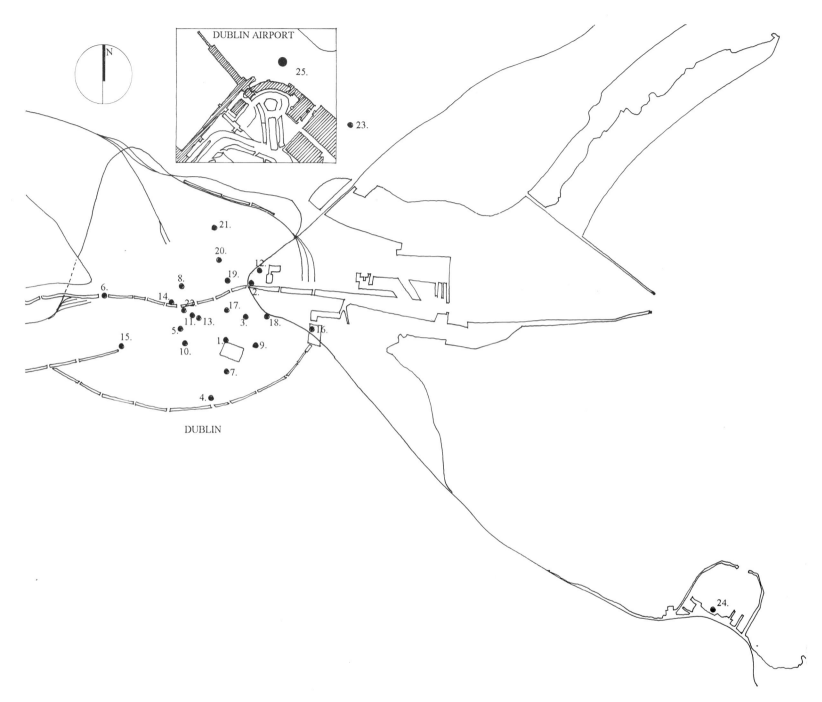

DUBLIN AIRPORT

DUBLIN

1. Grafton Street	6. Heuston Station	11. Dame Street	16. Grand Canal Dock	21. St. George's Church
2. Custom House	7. National Concert Hall	12. Busaras	17. College Green	22. Civic Offices, Wood Quay
3. Trinity College	8. Fruit and Vegetable Market	13. Dublin Castle	18. Westland Row	23. Casino at Marino
4. Portobello	9. Government Buildings	14. The Four Courts	19. O'Connell Street	24. Dún Laoghaire Harbour
5. Christchurch Cathedral	10. St. Patrick's Cathedral	15. Grand Canal Place	20, Rotunda, Parnell Street	25. Dublin Airport

Commentary by
Benedict Kiely

Grafton Street, 'the most fashionable street in Dublin', is as always a wonderful place for young and old. It has become more so since motor-traffic was barred therein, and the happy thousands can go it on foot and admire street performers and listen to street musicians.

Yet many people, I hope, will see there the ghost of a poet and hear him singing sadly about the lovely young woman he loved and lost:

In Grafton Street in November we tripped lightly along the ledge
Of the deep ravine where can be seen the worth of passion's pledge,
The Queen of Hearts still making tarts and I not making hay —
Oh I loved too much and by such by such is happiness thrown away.

The poet, as we all know, was Patrick Kavanagh. I had the honour of his friendship. I even knew the young lady he sang to and about.

One of Dublin's first pedestrian streets. Drawn from St Stephen's Green. April 1991.

In the far background and downstream on the Liffey is the Great Gasometer. Only one man did I ever meet who had been to the top of it. He told me that the view of Dublin therefrom was worth a million, and I could well believe him. But I never had the courage nor the opportunity to make the ascent.

But here's a story Brendan Behan told me. He and his dear wife Beatrice were coming home all the way via England and Wales from Paris: in the days when you sailed up the Liffey. So the lady looked ahead at James Gandon's most graceful Custom House, built in 1781, and very much part of the heart of her Dublin. Familiar to her as part of the vista from Butt Bridge, named after the great lawyer and statesman Sir Isaac Butt. She looked downstream over the busy Custom House Quay and asked: 'What is that strange building?' She meant the gasometer. She was informed. Then she said: 'I often wondered what it was.' And Brendan said: 'There you are. Travel broadens the mind.' One always thought that on Custom House Quay. The great dome soared aloft to Heaven. The great ships came and went. The world was out there.

Drawn from under the railway bridge. The gasometer has since been removed. April 1991.

Oliver Goldsmith and Edmund Burke stand with their backs to Trinity College. They are by no means renouncing the great school. They, poet and statesman, are proud of it for it helped to make them what they were. And you feel, when you enter through the arched gateway, into that most impressive campus, that you have entered there with their august permission.

Facing them from the opening of Dame Street is the gesturing figure of Henry Grattan, statesman and orator. They all belonged to the Dame world. Grattan gestures. Goldsmith makes notes in a little book. It was one of the many jests of that triple-headed man, Brian O'Nolan, Flann O'Brien or Myles na gCopaleen (call him what you will), that Grattan was passing on tic-tac tips for the horses and Goldsmith was jotting them down. Goldsmith might have been amused. Not so sure about Grattan.

Ah well, forget all that. Leave Dame Street where Mr W M Thackeray, as visitor from London, loved it and the lovely ladies he saw walking there. Go through the arched gateway into the reverend peace. Reverend and peaceful in spite of students and all that. Lecky, the historian, sits and surveys a learned place that the years can only fortify.

Early summer on the campus.
May 1991.

An area of the city
experiencing dereliction.
July 1991.

Several people of both sexes, or two I mean, I stopped on the streets of Dublin and asked them: 'If I said Portobello, what would you say to follow?'

One man said: 'Barracks.'

There was a famous barracks there in the days of Empire. It took the name from other and sunnier places. Changing fortunes changed the name to Cathal Brugha Barracks in memory of a good young man killed in the neighbourhood in the long, and continuing, struggle for Irish freedom from Empire.

I once heard a decent Dublin girl mispronounce it as 'Cattleboro Barracks'. Ah well! The Cattle Market was not, nor ever is, so far away.

There was also a bridge over the Grand Canal called Portobello Bridge. And there was, and is, Portobello harbour, where the Grand Canal barges, all the way from the Shannon, docked and released cargo and passengers. What a lovely pastoral way to travel. None of those mechanical voices roaring at you in airports.

There was also Portobello House, where the best passengers stayed in passing. It has been many things since then, but it is still there and as handsome as ever.

Gerald Griffin, the nineteenth-century novelist and more besides, travelled to Portobello all the way from Limerick. There were convicts on board going East for further accommodation. The barge moved slowly. But the convicts were in no hurry.

In every corner of an old city, or old town, or rural roadway, you are entitled to encounter the ghosts that you feel you know. And certainly around the great building of ancient Christchurch, on its high hill looking down on the Liffey, there are moments when the ghosts seem almost to take precedence over the living.

Think of even a few of the names: Strongbow and his clanking armoured men, the four Irish kings who were knighted and partially anglicised there in the fourteenth century. They were even introduced to 'trews' or trousers. Then there was poor Lambert Simnel who put on a crown there in 1487 but never had much opportunity to display it. On and on go the ghosts in pageant and procession.

But, oddly enough, when I walk under that magnificent arch and go down towards the Liffey water, the man I think of never clanked in armour nor uneasily wore a crown. The poet F R Higgins remembered him:

They'll miss his heavy stick and stride in Wicklow,
His story-talking down Winetavern Street,
Where old men sitting in the wizen daylight
Have kept an edge upon his gentle wit . . .

Yes, Pádraic Ó Conaire, storyteller, who turned his back on the present and wandered the past and the roads of Ireland, walked these streets.

Surrounded by nineteenth- and twentieth-century buildings. November 1991.

So I turn from the railway-station and the great bridge, and the rail and the river, and open an issue of Fr Senan's *The Capuchin Annual* for 1945–6, to study a series of splendid photographs collected under the title: 'A Contemporary Irish Master: Laurence Campbell RHA, at work on his statue of Seán Heuston.'

A splendid study of a great sculptor at work on the head and, you might say, the history of a man who gave his life for what he hoped would be the hopeful future of his country.

His countrymen also, in gratitude, gave his name to this fine railway-station gateway to the south and the southwest, as Amiens Street station became James Connolly station.

Formerly called Kingsbridge. After which King? I think I know. But it is amusing to set up a guessing game, or quiz show, about that.

Yet why bother? Salute the ghosts of long-gone kings. Bow to the young patriot. And take off on a fine modern train to see a lot of Ireland.

Drawn from Seán Heuston Bridge, just before the hoarding was removed from Dr Stephen's Hospital. November 1991.

Description of College: The College is outwardly a rectangular plain building with a fine porch where the mid-day sun pours down in Summer from the Donnybrook direction, heating the steps for the comfort of the students. The hallway inside is composed of large black and white squares arranged in the orthodox chessboard pattern, and the surrounding walls, done in an unpretentious cream wash, bear three rough smudges caused by the heels, buttocks and shoulders of the students.

The hall was crowded by students, some of them deporting themselves in a quiet civil manner. Modest girls bearing books filed in and out in the channels formed by the groups of boys. There was a hum of commerce and much bustle and activity . . .

That description was written down in *At Swim-Two-Birds* in the 1930s. It was Flann O'Brien, or Brian O'Nolan, or Myles na gCopaleen being irreverent, but not exactly inaccurate, about the scene in Main Hall, University College Dublin, in his time and my time.

Irreverent. Yet there's a gentle note in it. He has written from the heart about a place in which he and I, and many another, felt happy and at home. Many memorable encounters and meetings took place there and a little further to the east and in the Side Hall, close to the Physics Theatre.

And around the corner in St Stephen's Green were the ghosts of John Henry Newman, Gerard Manley Hopkins and James Joyce.

Then the campus moved south to the vast expanse of Belfield and the great God of Music took possession of Earlsfort Terrace.

26   The ghosts are still around the corner . . . listening.

Drawn sitting in
seat number F16, main balcony.
December 1991.

Morning activities at the market,
with the Civic Offices in the background.
February 1992.

To the bludgeons, good friends, or we are undone,
Butchers and Pen-Boys to our rescue come,
For you shall toil and slave no more,
No longer shall you wash our dishes, nor follow the swine,
As we shall train you in a band with clubs in hand,
If by us you will stand, and Clothe you very grand,
In garments of our donkeys, bullocks, swine and calves,
Armed to the teeth that you may save
Your own dear darling Smithfield lambs.

By the nature of things, there is always great company in the neighbourhood of markets. Sometimes, I hear you say, very mixed company. That odd, rough verse comes over the long years from a man now nameless and from a song or a poem or something called 'The Cry of the Monopolists: Smithfield Market'. James N Healy printed the whole harangue in his valuable *Mercier Book of Old Irish Ballads*. How any melody was ever tailored to suit the wild words I cannot imagine.

Oh, nothing at all to do with the clean, well-ordered markets of the present. Yet for men of my generation and the generations before and after, the markets meant the wonders and warmth and friendliness of Moore Street, and the fine face and ringing voice of Rosie, the Queen of Moore Street. A wonderful woman.

You walked round there from Radio Éireann, where, as a humorous Kerryman once said to me, 'everything happened in the attic in the GPO'. That was away before Teevee and Montrose.

You walked the stalls all laden with fruit and found a place to rest in Gerry Dwyer's pub, where you slaked your thirst, if you had one, and talked to friends and distinguished visitors, and thanked the Lord and Gerry Dwyer. Nelson was round the corner, still high on his pillar and 'watching his world collapse'. I could write a book about the men, and women, I met in the markets.

28

Up in the north of Dublin city and in a quiet little backwater, there may still be, if the trucks have not knocked it down, a modest little building, built for devotion to God, and known as the Black Church. The great poet Austin Clarke grew up in the neighbourhood. The local children had a comic superstition that if you ran thrice around the Black Church you saw the Devil.

So Austin called an enchanting portion of his autobiography 'Twice Round the Black Church'. He had no wish to meet that gentleman.

But what can we say about Government Buildings in Merrion Street, in magnificent Dublin South. Twice or thrice? The great circuit would include the National Art Gallery, Leinster House where our statesmen meet, the National Library and Stephen Dedalus still standing on the steps and talking, the ghost of the Kildare Street Club, and, leaving Trinity College to the left and turning right into Merrion Square, and passing again the National Art Gallery, and there you are.

No devils encountered.

But look at the past and think of some names: O'Connell, Wilde, Carson, Le Fanu, and many other ghosts.

Restored and saved for other generations.
March 1992.

We walk down the slope and irreverently approach St Patrick's Cathedral. Now here, at last, we may have found the true centre of Dublin. Forget about the Danes and forget about the wild Byrnes from Wicklow who felt that the fortress by the Black Pool should not be there.

But look at the exquisite old building and think of the dean. There have been several deans since Jonathan Swift. I had the honour of shaking the hand of one of them when he welcomed a group of journalists to the sacred precincts.

But forget about the present. Take a look into the past. The people who were here are looking at us.

Swift has sailed into his rest;
Savage indignation there
Cannot lacerate his breast.
Imitate him if you dare,
World-besotted traveller. He
Served human liberty.

Swift wrote that in Latin for all of us to read. Yeats turned it into those splendid lines. Great presences are here all around us. They come to pay homage to the spirit of Swift.

Little has changed since Malton's time.
March 1992.

32

Dublin's Grand Promenade nowadays would almost certainly be Grafton Street. It was always a fine street to walk along. But since the wheeled traffic was removed, and you are not liable to be knocked down by anything heavier than a street musician, it has become the ideal playground for the idle and the light of heart. Was it always so in Dublin?

Consider the route that Dame Street follows. Rattle down the hill from Christchurch and there you have it. Dublin Castle, once a fortress, to the right. And the old City Hall. Olympia Theatre to the left and echoes of Jimmy O'Dea and Harry O'Donovan. And the ghosts of Commercial Buildings and the Ouzel Gallery, and the merry Ringsend sailingmen who said they had been nailed by pirates but came home suspiciously loaded with booty.

Banks and fine buildings all around you. To the left again what was once the Houses of Parliament. And the Royal Bank of Ireland and the Bank of Ireland. And Tom Moore making melodies on a pedestal. And Trinity College staring you in the face.

There's a promenade!

Heavy traffic on a Saturday morning.
May 1992.

Can any man over the age of seventy look at that splendid Busaras building and not recall the first time he was ever in a Bus? How many of you away out there are over seventy? Long silence. No answer. Ah well! Ashamed to admit it.

My own first bus took me, some time back, from Omagh to Drumquin and the 'Hills above Drumquin'.

God bless the hills of Donegal,
I've heard their praises sung
In days gone by, beyond recall
When I was very young,
Then I would pray I'd live to see
Before life's course was run,
When I would sing the praises
Of the Hills above Drumquin.

A great song. Written by Felix Kearney. I had the honour of meeting him when he was over seventy and not ashamed of it.

But about that first bus. The driver, and conductor (that word had not then been invented except by Julius Caesar or somebody who had run into him), was a man called Crane. He was six feet tall . . .

Jane, Jane, tall as a crane,
The morning light creaks down again.

Some poet, help us all, wrote that. And Crane, in the bus, was so tall he could not stand up straight in the wee rattly Bus. What a word! It almost meant a kiss.

Then I came to Dublin. The tram was in control. I could write a book about trams. Stop me. James Joyce did his best.

But a new sort of bus was taking over. Smooth gliding, comfortable, and two storeys (floors) to it. And from that great building they now issue forth to conquer Ireland.

36

Three layers of architectural history: Amiens Street Station, Busaras and the Financial Services Centre. November 1992.

Many of us, over a certain age and with our origins in rural Ireland, found our reference to Dublin Castle in the pages of a periodical produced by the Irish Christian Brothers and called *Our Boys.* What a collection! The Boys, I mean.

But there was once in those pages a most moving serial-story about Red Hugh O'Donnell of the ships, the chief whom nothing daunted, and about how, in his boyhood, he and a few friends were cheated into captivity and conveyed, by sea and land, to Dublin Castle. And about how they escaped, in mid-winter, to the friendship and safety of the Wicklow Mountains.

One fragment of the narrative stays forever in my memory: 'Art O'Neill was fat and could not travel fast . . .' Then O'Donnell headed north-west and through O'Neill country, where I was later to live, and to his home and fortress in Tír Chonaill. West Tyrone where, and when, I grew up. And you could almost see him pass.

And then, at about the age of ten, I was first brought to Dublin, and the first thing I had to see was the Castle. It has changed, I'd say, over the centuries. But I have my own way of looking at it.

Recently restored and extended by the Office of Public Works. June 1992.

Fort of the Dane,
Garrison of the Saxon,
Augustan capital
Of a Gaelic nation,
Appropriating all
The alien brought,
You give me time for thought
And by a juggler's tricks
You poise the toppling hour —
O greyness run to flower,
Grey stone, grey water
And brick upon grey brick.

That was the great poet and Ulsterman, Louis MacNeice, putting down some of his thoughts on Dublin city, where he was a much admired man. He knew many cities, and many good people therein knew and admired him.

His words beat back at you as you walk around any of the great historic buildings that have been for so long the centres of activity. And where can men be more active than around the Courts of Law. And then the history of the place from the time when one of James Gandon's masterpieces grew up, against difficulties, out of the rubble of the past to the time when it faced ruin and bloodshed in a civil war.

Restoration followed, and the great business goes on.

Drawn sitting in a car during off-peak traffic.
March 1993.

A timespan scene of
Dublin's modern industry
and its industrial archaeology.
March 1993.

The chisellers bent perilously over the parapet, heels kicking, used to shout: 'Mister, bring us back a monkey.' Sometimes the wish, or demand, was for a parrot. And once I heard an original who had, clearly, read *Treasure Island*, demanding a chest of gold.

All that was when a Guinness barge, bringing the good stuff downstream to the big seagoing ship, ducked the steaming funnel to pass under O'Connell Bridge. Then, when the sad day came and the riverside truck replaced the barge, Tom Collins and Charlie Kelly of *Dublin Opinion* paid a most moving tribute. There, in their drawing, in black and white, he stood on a barge, the great Boss of the Great Brewery. And Lord Tennyson was called on for the words:

And slowly answered Arthur from the barge:
The Old Order changeth, yielding place to New . . .

All that was on the River Liffey. But, also, on the two great canals the day of the barge and of the canals was ending.

Two great canals? Some people might say: Panama and Suez. Or some other names elsewhere. In hyperborean regions some might raise a claim for the Newry. But here in Dublin we meant the Grand and the Royal.

One can no longer, here in Dublin, think of canals without rightaway quoting Patrick Kavanagh and remembering that scholar and gentleman, John Ryan.

For the poet (I often told him and he did not disagree), St Stephen's Green could have been the Fair Green in a country town. Baggot Street was Main Street and the canal bridge was, as the song said, 'the bridge below the town'.

On a bench by the water he sat and thought, and wrote. He still sits there, thanks, in the beginning to John Ryan, then to the poet's brother and to a fine group of people remembering Patrick and John: and to the sculptor John Coll.

O commemorate me where there is water,
Canal water preferably, so stilly
Green at the heart of summer. Brother
Commemorate me thus beautifully.
Where by a lock niagarously roars
The falls for those who sit in the tremendous silence
Of mid-July. No one will speak in prose
Who finds his way to these Parnassian islands.
A swan goes by head low with many apologies,
Fantastic light looks through the eyes of bridges —
And look! a barge comes bringing from Athy
And other far-flung towns mythologies.
O commemorate me with no hero-courageous
Tomb — just a canal-bank seat for the passer-by.

The Inland Waterways Visitor Centre in the setting of the Grand Canal basin. May 1993.

There's a charm that dwells above you
In your guardian mountains grand.
There's a charm that's close beside you
In the green, surrounding land.
There's a charm that lies before you
In the ever restless sea,
By its presence there attesting
You were destined to be free.

Every charm proclaims a city
That should be a nation's pride.
Not a slave whose claim for justice
May be mocked or cast aside.
Now we pray the hour approaches
That will see you win your claim,
That will see you rise in freedom,
In prosperity and fame . . .

Walking the other day from the City Hall and the corner of Parliament Street to talk to Thomas Moore in College Green, I found myself quoting those fine lines in praise of Dublin. And asking myself who wrote them. And then finding myself unable to answer that question. All I knew was that I came across them in Maureen Jolliffe's *The Third Book of Irish Ballads* (Mercier Press, 1970). The good anthologist rightly praised the lines which come to us pleasantly from some lyrical Unknown.

And the lines measure your steps and lift your heart as you walk towards what has to be the centre of Dublin: College Green. Everybody seems to be there: on the pavement and on pedestals.

There will be arguments about that. A great city may have many centres. But many people will agree with me. Thomas Moore did when I asked him. In defiance of Leopold Bloom. And Moore must have had his influence on the person who wrote those fine lines. And also, perhaps, Thomas Davis.

One of the more difficult drawings to complete due to interruptions by large numbers of passers-by. February 1994.

46

Sixty-five years ago I knew I was in Dublin when I first laid eyes on Moran's Hotel. In those days, if you travelled any distance at all, you travelled by train. And outside every railway-station there were great illustrated hoardings telling you of the delights awaiting you in the City. So when I first crossed the Boyne and got as far as Amiens Street (Connolly Station) and came down the steep steps and was led as far as the corner of Talbot Street and Gardiner Street, I knew where I was. From that moment on, Dublin's railway-stations held a magic for me.

The very name of Westland Row seemed to imply that you were off on a splendid journey. Like Columbus himself. Or was it an echo of Charles Kingsley's Westward Ho? And Westland Row itself, when discovered, was a stylish street for strollers. A station, a school, a fine hotel, an association with the name of Pearse. And more.

Later on in years, when I had the honour and privilege of becoming a friend of Brinsley MacNamara, that promenade acquired an added significance. Brinsley liked to walk in stately fashion in the Row. He was then secretary of the National Gallery, where I would call for him. Then an inspection of the books in Greene's. Then round two corners and into the Row. Down all the way and up again. A brief pause in Kennedy's for a sip and a bit of philosophy. Then round another corner and via Lincoln Place to take the air on the green ground of Trinity College. To salute Lecky, the great historian, and to emerge between Goldsmith and Burke. And Brinsley talking of Delvin and the midlands and his memories. No brains could have brought me on a more instructive journey.

One of the few wet days depicted. February 1994.

Oisín Kelly's 'Jim Larkin'
and Francis Johnston's General Post Office.
February 1994.

Come gather round me, players all,
Come praise Nineteen Sixteen,
Come from the pit or gallery
Or from the painted scene,
Who fought in the Post Office,
Or round the City Hall,
Praise every man that came again,
Praise every man that fell.
From mountain to mountain
Ride the fierce horsemen.

That, as you may already have guessed, was the Great Poet,
William Yeats, remembering, as he did in other lines and in
splendid style, what had happened in the main street of Dublin
in 1916. To the left of the picture is the General Post Office
where the valiant men took their stand against the stupidities of
British imperialism: that one town should own and run the
world.

Well, all that has long passed. But the restored Post Office is
still with us.

And raising his heroic arms over the street is James Larkin, the
great Labour leader who stood up, against the bosses, for the
workers and the poor.

Early Sunday morning.
March 1994.

At the northern extremity, or beginning, all depending on which way you are going, of O'Connell Street, formerly Sackville Street, there are three notable monuments.

One is the Rotunda Maternity, or Lying-In Hospital, from which so much of life comes forth into the city. One can hear the echoes of the names of such great men as Dr Bethel Solomons.

And there is the Gate Theatre, not quite visible in our picture, for so long involved with and still cherishing the names of Lord and Lady Longford.

The third monument, quite visible, is the obelisk to the memory of that fine statesman and patriot, Charles Stewart Parnell:

For Parnell was a proud man,
No prouder trod the ground,
And a proud man's a lovely man,
So, pass the bottle round.

Once again, the voice of Yeats.

But Dublin like all cities or other gatherings of human beings has its own irreverent jokes. Underneath Parnell are written in gold some of his great words: 'No man may set a boundary to the onward march of a nation.' He raises his right hand. He points exactly to a famous bar a little to the west and along the street which also bears his name.

TO
CHARLES STEWART PARNELL

NO MAN HAS A RIGHT TO FIX
THE BOUNDARY OF THE MARCH
OF A NATION NO MAN HAS A
RIGHT TO SAY TO HIS COUNTRY
THUS FAR SHALT THOU GO AND
NO FURTHER WE HAVE NEVER
ATTEMPTED TO FIX THE NE PLUS
ULTRA TO THE PROGRESS OF
IRELAND'S NATIONHOOD AND
WE NEVER SHALL

The SEAGULL

The opening years of the nineteenth century saw, Maurice Craig tells us: 'the initiation (1802) and completion (1814) of St George's Church and of the General Post Office, both by Francis Johnston.'

St George's, he tells us, was an example of a tendency, 'typical of classical urbanism but till then notable in Dublin by its absence, the placing of prominent buildings, and especially churches, at the terminations of vistas or at their intersections. St Stephen's is another, and so, a little later, is Rathmines church and the Presbyterian church at the head of Earlsfort Terrace (1840)'.

Ernest Renan wrote splendidly about the legend in Brittany of the supposed City of Is that was said to have been swallowed by the sea but to reappear on stormy days and even send out the sound of bells. Anatole France commented that it seemed to him that he had in the depth of his heart a City of Is 'whose bells will not cease from ringing as they call to the sacred offices the faithful who no longer heed their summons. Sometimes I pause to listen to these tremulous vibrations which seem to steal upon my inward ears from unfathomable depths, like voices from anther world'.

Ah well! Temple Street has its own angel voices in the famous Maternity Hospital.

As another famous writer said:

Twould ring the Bells of Heaven
The wildest peal for years . . .

Licence was taken in omitting the scaffolding that surrounds this fine church by Francis Johnston.
April 1994.

Perhaps it was one of the necessities of modern progress that a station should be built upon the site of the mouldering Cour des Comptes of pleasant memory; that the trees should be uprooted from our quays; that underground trains and steam tramways should make their ways along this once-peaceful riverside . . .

No. There, as you will have observed, we were not in Dublin. But off in Paris, France, and many years ago, and in the company of Anatole France who dearly loved and eloquently wrote about that splendid city. Let him continue. He accepted the mingling of old and new as a fine sign of continuing life:

It is there that I am warmed with the tenderest and most whole-hearted affection for the land of my birth, and there it is borne in upon me that it is the mission of Paris to be a light to lighten the world . . .

And here in Dublin, and in one eyeful, we have the splendid new Civic Offices and the ancient Christchurch Cathedral. Just think: Maurice Craig reminds us that round about the time of the Battle of Aughrim in July 1691, King James heard Mass in Christchurch — 'the tabernacle and candlesticks are still shown in the crypt'.

The drawing was completed before the building. The architect's designs were referred to for accuracy. May 1994.

When a boy from the provinces who had gone to school to the Irish Christian Brothers heard mention of the Casino at Marino, he might have wondered if the good Brothers at their great house in Marino were going in for gambling. Not so. But the comic notion made one, visiting Dublin in the early years, look with wonder on the exquisite buildings and anxious to learn its history, as explained by Maurice Craig in his most valuable volume, *The Architecture of Ireland: From the Earliest Times to 1880* (Batsford).

Dr Craig wrote of the decade 1758–68 as of crucial importance to the history of Dublin architecture. He gives the details, and adds: 'By 1762, being then 34 years of age, Lord Charlemont had decided that his duty required him to live in Ireland, and more particularly in Dublin, where he presently built Charlemont House in the Rotunda Gardens, and the Casino at Clontarf, a little distance away, both designed by Sir William Chambers and bringing to Dublin extremely advanced and refined examples of Franco-Roman neo-classic taste.'

The return of Malton's man and pig.
May 1994.

Initial drawings were produced
while sitting on a boat in the harbour.
July 1993.

O Bay of Dublin, my heart you are troublin',
Your beauty haunts me like a fevered dream.
Like frozen fountains that the sun sets bubblin'
My heart's blood warms when I but hear your name.

So Helen Selina, Lady Dufferin, wrote and she wrote a lot and
well. And I have heard the lines sung in places in Dublin the
like of which were never frequented by Lady Dufferin. Stephen
Behan, the father of Brendan, could quote it with great style
and affection for his city:

Sweet Wicklow mountains! The sunlight sleeping
On your green banks is a picture rare.
You crowd around me like young girls peeping
And puzzling me to say which is most fair.

My own first vision of the bay and the proud sails of the yachts
came from the Bull Wall, and later on another vision from the
legendary Hill of Howth. Then to the south and Killiney
Strand, the hill above it, when it was good to be able to shout
aloud Francis A Fahy's song:

To Killiney, far away, flies my fond heart night and day
To ramble bright and happy through its fields and dells.
For here life smiles in vain, and earth's a land of pain
While all that's bright in Erin in Killiney dwells . . .

It's a love song and with a touch of melancholy. But the lines
seemed to go with the dance of the white sails and one came to
regard with joy and reverence the busy harbour and the Yacht
Club.

Terminal building.
Special permission was required
to work on the apron.
November 1993.

There rolls the deep where grew a tree,
O Earth! What changes hast thou seen,
There where the long street roars, has been
The stillness of the Central Sea . . .

There are the style of majestic lines you quote, or misquote, from memory. And I mutter them to myself, or shout them aloud, depending on the company I am in, when I travel out along what used to be known as the Swords Road.

It may have many names now. For, half ways to Swords and if you swing left, or turn round and round, you end up in the great International Airport.

Years back, and not so many years, you went to Swords if you lived there or had business there, or wished to walk and take the air in the green paradise of north County Dublin. By night, if you were thirsty, you could slip out to two or three notable houses 'in the place called Swords on an Irish road, it is told for our renown'. There I am, quoting G K Chesterton in a ballad he wrote about the Labour troubles in the 1920s . . .

Then Dublin city spread out and everybody, and not only military men, took to the air. And that was that. But it is wonderful, and perverse, to walk in the great airport and remember green walks all the way to Malahide Island and other places.

There's a lot of history on the Swords Road.